Vanishing Act

DATE DUE

AN 1 4 2011

Vanishing Act

The Erosion of Online Footnotes and Implications for Scholarship in the Digital Age

By Michael Bugeja and Daniela V. Dimitrova

Litwin Books, LLC
Duluth, Minnesota

Published in 2010

Published by Litwin Books, LLC
P.O. Box 3320
Duluth, MN 55803
http://litwinbooks.com/

This book is printed on acid-free paper that meets present ANSI standards for archival preservation.

Library of Congress Cataloging-in-Publication Data

Bugeja, Michael J.
 Vanishing act : the erosion of online footnotes and
implications for scholarship in the digital age / by
Michael Bugeja and Daniela V. Dimitrova.
      p. cm.
 Includes bibliographical references and index.
 ISBN 978-1-936117-14-7 (acid-free paper)
1. Citation of electronic information resources--
Evaluation. I. Dimitrova, Daniela V. II. Title.
 PN171.F56B84 2010
 808'.027--dc22

      2010006380

For Mikayle and Philip

Contents

Acknowledgements

The authors wish to acknowledge Samuel Berbano, Michael Bugeja's research assistant, as well as previous research assistants Hye-Hyun Hong, Erin O'Gara, and Elizabeth Geske in helping to compile data presented in this work. Contents of this book include language and data that may have appeared in the authors' previous research published in *American Communication Journal, Journalism and Mass Communication Educator, Iowa Journal of Communication, New Media & Society, portal: Libraries and the Academy* and *The Serials Librarian*. We acknowledge those journals and their editors for publishing original versions of our research in different format and text. This book represents an attempt to update and re-assemble the mosaic of our research into a cohesive argument to understand the impact of vanishing footnotes on scholarship and the implications for researchers now and in the future.

Chapter 1

Extinct Citations, Missing Links and Other Bibliographical Wonders

A decade ago, most research was done in the library rather than through its Web site, and scholars, editors, graduate directors and librarians were meticulous about the integrity of footnotes. They knew that citation was the backbone of research, from agronomy to zoology in the sciences and from art history to Zen studies in the humanities. The footnote upheld standards because it allowed others to test hypotheses or replicate experiments. Testing and replication are at the heart of the peer review and scientific processes upon which academe is based, from papers by first-year and transfer students to grants by postdoc and professor.

Because so much depended on the foundation of all scholarship, the footnote, academicians admonished students for sloppy or erroneous citation. This was the norm even a decade ago when most research was done in the library rather than through its Web site. Our discipline of communication scholarship was as exacting as any other in the academy, especially when it came to footnotes. Students submitting dissertations and faculty, journal articles, were fastidious about the accuracy of footnotes, knowing that their reputations relied on the fine print at the bottom of the page or at the end of the manuscript. Unacceptable were citations that simply named the source without specifying the document, as in "U.S. Mint, 801 9th Street NW, Washington, DC 20220-0001." The worst types of mistakes would contain particulars, including an article's title and date of publication, but might locate it in the wrong volume and issue of a journal. Indeed, if dissertation advisers went to the stacks to verify citations, as they often did, they would be aghast at checking a citation and finding none in any volume or number, or finding it with wrong pages or other particulars, and discovering a journal with those pages ripped out and missing. Those mistakes could doom a letter of recommendation for a job or advanced study.

Now scholars don't worry so much about footnotes. The emphasis in the Internet age has been more on access to data rather than retrieval thereof, with academics promoting that access via technology initiatives that have all but transformed some university libraries into computer centers with gourmet coffee rather than learning centers with expert archivists. The phenomenon of vanishing citations seems more like a techno-logical glitch—a downed server or corrupt file—than a lapse in methodology. The typical student, professor and researcher now seems to overlook the disappearance of primary sources in an article or a document, rather than questioning where those sources went or trying to recover them, merely because the Internet glitches so frequently, that the convenience of online research would be severely undermined, if we kept our meticulous ways. As we will learn, the tilt toward convenience over substance has put at risk peer review and scientific proc-ess upon which research, invention and innovation have been based since the Enlightenment.

Indeed, Davis[1] argues that convenience may play a role in the increasing popularity of online citations. Our research pivots on three time-tested aspects of accountable scholar-ship:

---

[1] Davis, Philip. "Effect of the Web on Undergraduate Citation Behavior: Guiding Student Scholarship in a Networked Age." *Libraries and the Academy* 3, no. 1 (2003): 41–51.

- *Text must be stabilized.* Researchers must have access to original documents rather than manipulated versions thereof.
- *Citations in those documents must be retrievable.* Researchers must have access to archives that guarantee both the longevity of technical formats and cited URLs.
- *The digital library must remain a repository of fact as much as a dissemination point of information.* The emphasis on the latter has eroded the former so that no universal archive exists to ensure the permanency associated with the scientific tradition.

The digital library is an oasis of convenience rather than an oasis of escape for the curious mind. With the advent of easily accessible data from a library open online at all hours, citation mistakes are common and routinely overlooked. This is not to say that footnotes are out of fashion; quite the contrary, if you analyze the implosion of citation in scholarly articles or conference papers. Citation indices in library databanks or on Google Scholar are gauges of how influential a professor's work has been over time. In fact, it is easier than ever to cite an online source with the select, copy and paste function of the typical computer. It only makes sense that footnoting sources would become more plentiful in the digital age because the platforms have multiplied. American Psychological Association style, for instance, has formats for articles from online periodicals; online periodicals with assigned digital object identifiers (bar codes); articles from a database; digital abstracts; electronic newspaper articles; electronic books; sections of Web documents or online book chapters; online book reviews, dissertations and theses from a database; online encyclopedias and dictionaries; online bibliographies and annotated bibliographies; digital data sets; interactive maps and other graphic representations of data; qualitative data and online interviews; online lecture notes and presentation slides; non-periodical Web documents; Web pages or reports; computer software and downloaded software; e-mail; online forum or discussion board postings; blogs (weblog) and video blog posts; wikis; and audio and video podcasts. We have become more meticulous about identifying the digital source rather than fact-checking to see if it has vanished.

There is no question that Internet and other digital technologies and applications are fabulous resources for quick and easy source material used in footnotes. But new media platforms and applications are abysmal when it comes to later retrieval, primarily because text and graphics accumulate in a device, server or databank, and those are the domains (literally and figuratively) of computer science whose god is the server and file system, the angelic orders. There is no history or tradition associated with libraries that honors these deities the way that librarians used to honor fact in the archival repository. New librarians are apt to be digital natives skilled in social networks but may forget why they should be fastidious about fact. Our book challenges them as well as information and computer scientists whose god is the file folder rather than the book shelf. This study continues to challenge advocates of online scholarship to stop touting the convenience of easy access and start resolving issues of later retrieval. Despite what literary natives know about the importance of reliable footnotes in literature reviews and scientific protocols—especially in the medical arts—academia has looked askance at suggestions that footnote accuracy must be maintained if the integrity of scholarship is to endure. Our book asks "why." *Why should Internet-based scholarship be less trustworthy than that of the paper-era?* We also want to know the four other "W"s and "H":

- When do Internet citations disappear?
- Where do disappearing citations go?
- Who is responsible for preserving them?
- What can be done to lengthen the lifespan of those citations?
- How can that be achieved?

We began our exploration of this phenomenon more than seven years ago when co-author Michael Bugeja, writing a book about Internet, no less, checked his citations before submitting his manuscript to Oxford University Press, and discovered that almost half of his Web citations had vanished. This was 2003, and Bugeja and research partner and co-author Daniela Dimitrova had not yet considered the phenomenon. Literary natives, both were aghast at the implications for scholarship in the digital age. Bugeja had to inform his editor that delivery of *Interpersonal Divide: The Search For Community in a Technological Age* would be delayed for weeks while he searched for missing URLs and made photocopies of every citation, to prove the accuracy of his citations, if ever challenged. Meanwhile, Dimitrova researched the effect of "link-rot" in library science. One early chronicler of the effect was the Web Surveying Team at the Georgia Institute of Technology, which reported lapsed URLs in a survey[2]. About the time we noticed the impact of lapsed footnotes, a study was published examining Internet footnotes in *New England Journal of Medicine*, *The Journal of the American Medical Association* and *Sci-*

---

[2] "GVU's Eighth WWW User Survey: Problems Using the Web Graphs." http://www.cc.gatech.edu/gvu/user_surveys/survey-1997-10/graphs/use/Problems_Using_the_Web.html. 24 Oct 2009.

ence, noting that after two years, 13% of online references were
inaccessible[3].

That is how our journey began, and here for the time being,
it will end, with our sounding a warning on how vanishing
footnotes over time will result in ever unreliable literature reviews and follow-up studies; be the cause of failed experiments in the hard and medical sciences because data of previous studies no longer can be retrieved; and seriously erode the
methodology of history and media history whose research
procedures rely more than any other discipline on accurate
citation.

Our several studies, synopsized here and expanded in this
book, contain new data, analyses and discussion. We warn that
the decay of footnotes threatens the very tradition of peer
review upon which degrees are conferred, articles published,
and knowledge advanced. As such, our research has a historical component. In *The Footnote: A Curious History,* Princeton
historian Anthony Grafton observes that citations, especially
in scientific (and, by extension, *social* science) works, contain a
compendium of information, such as the intellectual culture
of an academic program, the pedagogical methods of its
graduate students, and the editorial preferences of its journal[4].
Intellectual culture, pedagogical methods, and editorial preferences are precisely what the current academic generation
stands to lose if the phenomenon of disappearing online citations continues. The only prevailing culture will be the most
current evolving one; the pedagogical method will be on what
can be accessed in the current moment; and the editorial pref-

---

[3] Dellavalle, Robert et al. "Going, Going, Gone: Lost Internet
References." *Science* 302, no. 5646 (2003): 787-788.
[4] Grafton, Anthony. *The Footnote: A Curious History.* Cambridge,
MA: Harvard University Press, 1999.

erences will be those listed on the current masthead. This book will document comprehensively how that scenario is likely to result if editors continue to overlook deteriorating digital citations.

   This book also looks at where we started with what we call the "half-life" effect, or how long it typically takes for one half of online citations in a journal to vanish from the Web. Through a methodology that we adapted and perfected over the past several years, analyzing data on individual articles, we can project with reasonable precision when the half-life will occur for an entire journal. We measure how many footnotes have lapsed in each article published in each edition of a journal over the course of a year. That not only gives us an idea of the scope of the linkrot but also a general view of the phenomenon over time. Once the data are retrieved for one journal, we can compare that with others in the same genre, giving an overall view that might yield anything from best and worst editing practices to comparisons of communications journals with those of other disciplines. Compiling data over a period of years makes the half-life phenomenon a more salient issue. Typically in books such as this research methodologies are omitted for the sake of reader interest, because the diction of scholarly analysis is dense; however, we include the methodology in an appendix so that other researchers interested in the half-life effect can document, replicate and advance the preservation of citation. As such, this book also chronicles where we came in our research and what conclusions we can share with other scholars to address the half-life issue. Specifically, we have tracked down the use of online citations by scholars in our discipline over a four-year period and examined the rate of decay of those citations, enabling us to estimate a half-life for online citations in journalism and communication journals. That figure is important in assessing the half-life phenomenon over time. For instance, if editors know the half-life in advance, they can take steps to mitigate its effects, following advice the authors provide later in this book, and then chart the rate of decay to see if it has slowed or quickened since the last analysis. Collectively, then, half-life estimations shared later in this work can be compared with new rates of decay for the same journals in private studies by editors or by communication scholars. In sum, for all these reasons, we opted to reprint the methodology in Appendix A.

It is high time for scholars not only in our disciplines but in the entire academy to understand the half-life phenomenon and the risks associated with online sources. Vanishing online footnotes undermine the building blocks of research, and their disappearance raises concerns about the reliability and replicability of scholarship. That fact alone—replicability—undermines the foundation of peer review, for without footnotes tracking back to accessible sources, the scientific method becomes impossible. No one person is responsible for that method as it evolved alongside the history of science. Its fundamental form is to ask a question, research what has been written about that or similar questions (literature review), formulate a hypothesis, create a methodology to test the hypothesis, collect findings, analyze and discuss data, and posit some conclusions. Publication is a part of that scientific method, for without dissemination of data, so that others may scrutinize hypotheses, findings and/or conclusions, we lack the requisite component of replicability. A study has to be accessible over time for its assertions to be proved correct, partially correct, or wrong. Consequently, the entire infrastructure of this method on which we have based centuries of progress is built on the foundation of the footnote; otherwise, we research on shifting sand, an apt metaphor for the half-life effect.

In science and medicine, this effect could literally be a life-and- death matter. The inability to replicate the research of others would undermine the foundations of scientific research as it has been known. When citations in medical databanks lapse, physicians must search for missing footnotes using the Wayback Machine, which compiles snapshots of the Web at regular time frames, or hunt for missing sources using other Internet tools, all the while making sure to access an identical version of the vanished text. The process takes time that otherwise could be devoted to experimentation, especially as online citations in leading medical journals tend to lapse at a rate of 13 percent over 27 months[5]. In the humanities and social sciences, where the stakes might not be life and death, the entire research enterprise is nonetheless threatened in the same way when citations and even texts turn to vapor[6]. Worse, the academic tradition is being violated, especially in literature reviews, because one study that should be linked theoretically or methodologically to another, no longer can be, because of vanishing links. As a result, studies cannot build upon each other for richer literature reviews and deeper analyses. It was therefore critical for us to inquire whether this phenomenon was being addressed by the people disseminating the data: journal editors. Their views will be shared later in this book, providing additional insights into the challenges associated with Internet citation. Later we also will provide other precautions that scholars can take until online information is stabilized so as to preserve the integrity of peer review and scientific method.

---

[5] Dellavalle et al.

[6] Nardini, Bob. "Invisible Links." *Academia: An Online Magazine and Resource for Academic Librarians* (2005). http://www.ybp.com/acad/features/0705_bugeja.html. 26 Aug 2009.

Specifically, the present book focuses on nine leading journals in the area of journalism and communication. Using longitudinal data and a content analysis methodology, we analyzed the use of online footnotes in refereed journal articles over a four-year period (2000-2003). We could have continued our data analyses into 2008 (and perhaps beyond); but we were less interested in charting recent vanishings and more interested in documenting when citations first began to lapse, showing the acceleration to the point where the half-life could be predicted. We were equally as interested in charting the effect in traditional vs. new media journals of communication, to see if content about digital platforms also resulted in more lapsed citations; then we wanted to compare those data with that of media history journals, as the latter's primary methodologies all assume footnote reliability. In sum, we found it more useful to publish findings from our own historical perspective as one of the first research teams to study the effect and the only communication-based team to do so in depth. As such this book builds upon and extends our previous work.

Chapter 2

Internet's Coming of Age – the Stone Age, That Is - As Far As Citation

The noun "archive" means a collection of records usually in a physical place, such as a library or warehouse, which must be visited to be checked out or analyzed; in the case of Internet, archive usually means files on a server that can be accessed via user identification and password. Archives are as old as caves. Our ancient ancestors recorded their cultural histories there in pictorial etchings. Millennia passed without much archival advancement. Then, sometime in the 3rd millennium BC, someone had the idea of storing records on clay tablets in the Babylonian temple of Nippur, one of the earliest archives[7]. Modern museum-goers know that clay tablets can be read to this day because sun-baked clay is nearly imperishable. In this manner humankind's record keepers unintentionally created three criteria of archives, which remained unchanged until the Internet age: *place, implement,* and *material.* If you were the archivist in Nippur, your place would have been a temple; your implement, a quill; and your material, wet clay to be sun-dried after etching into tablets. Later, in Western culture, the archivist would move from the Greek temples of the 4th century BC to the repositories of Alexandria and Pergamum. By then, the clay tablet was an outdated platform, yielding to the innovation of papyrus, vellum, parchment, and paper.

What, precisely, was driving innovation back then? The answer is the same as today's: *convenience.* Throughout history,

---

[7] "Library." *The New Encyclopaedia Britannica.* 15th ed. Chicago: Encyclopaedia Britannica: 333.

concerning archives, convenience trumped permanence when
it came to fetching something from the archives. Convenience
is to portability as permanence is to durability. Clay was more
convenient to carry and contained more information than du-
rable stone. Scrolls contained more data than tablets and were
more portable, too. Hand-written books were more portable
and lengthier than scrolls, and printed books were more portable and lengthier still[8]. You get the idea. However, there were
some features of archives that remained the same from the
mid 15th to the late 20th centuries: place (library), implement
(inked printing press), and material (paper). Moreover, the
library owned the products of the printing press. The Internet
scrambled all these factors, making physical place insignificant
with 24/7 accessible databanks and digital journals and books,
owned by others and stored as files on servers.

Convenience still drives library science when it comes to
access. In essence, it changed the purpose of the library from
an archive of records to the vender of somebody else's records that may or may not be retrievable at a later date. Librarians are recalling a time when they were more important
than computer programmers and are trying "to preserve online scholarly journals, saying they could vanish into oblivion
should publishers go out of business or face other calamities,"
(Kaufman) especially since libraries do not own and store content of journals licensed in electronic form. At the heart of
vanishing footnotes, then, are the Internet's obliteration of
place and material. *There is no there there in cyberspace.* In the past
the archivist knew the implement and material, from stick on
wet clay to ink on paper; now, however, the implement of the
computer over the past few decades in its various forms and

---

[8] Rychkov, Cheryl. "Medieval Manuscript Production." 2003.
http://library.rmwc.edu/hours/production.html. 10 Mar 2006.

reincarnations (desktop to iPhone) not only are incompatible with each other, but also with each new generation of software (from XyWrite to InCopy). All these factors propelled the Janus-faced digital library into the innovative future, as far as convenience of access was concerned, and into the stone age as far as later retrieval was concerned. It may be easier, in fact, to retrieve stone age documents from an archeologist's dig than to retrieve a file from a 1981 portable Osborne 1 computer weighing 24.5 pounds with 64K RAM and a 5-inch built-in monitor, for example. Unlike the Stone Age, however, scholars in modern times—as did those in the days of Aristotle and Alexandria—still need reliable archives to retrieve content that endures over time. Without it, the implications for research are dire.

When the Internet came of age many scholars commented on its positive effects for research development. Using the global network, academics, for example, could access articles written by other academics, through the digital library, the open source databank, and the personal or institutional Web site. Scientists, social scientists and humanists would not have to travel to remote towns or distant cities, just to secure primary sources—diaries, letters, journals, photographs, lab reports, diagnoses, research protocols and the like; they could simply use the desktop computer at home or at work to enter library databases, journals or indices. Research productivity skyrocketed, mainly because scholars could remain in one place at all hours to do work rather than traveling to a library, say, and honoring that institution's hours of operation. Users of the Internet set their own hours, and soon enough, their own rules.

Students began to set their own hours and rules, too. One of the first phenomena of the Internet age was the spike in plagiarism. Not only could students introduced to the global village locate research through an easy, quick online search; they could select, copy and paste what they wanted from the digital library or databank into their home or laptop computer. Many failed to realize that downloading copy and calling it yours, merely because they filed it in a folder called "My Documents," didn't, in fact, mean that they created the documents. In sum, it was easier to steal rather than cite words. One of the first publications to call students on this was the venerable New York Times, an oft-cited and plagiarized source available through most public and institutional libraries. The Times reported results of a study conducted on 23 college campuses, finding that Internet plagiarism was rising. Some 38% of undergraduate students surveyed admitted "that in the last year they had engaged in one or more instances of 'cut-and-paste' plagiarism involving the Internet, paraphrasing or copying anywhere from a few sentences to a full paragraph from the Web without citing the source"[9]. More startling was the fact that almost half the students believed cut-and-paste plagiarism was "trivial" and not really cheating. A similar survey three years earlier, in 2000, revealed that only 10 percent of students had acknowledged that plagiarism was, in fact, cheating. Worse, some academics supported this notion because they believed access to the Internet was more important than later retrieval and that cracking down on word theft inhibited innovation and engagement. Others, such as Susan D. Blum, an anthropologist at Notre Dame, has written that plagiarism is more of a cultural than ethical issue, noting that few academics take time to calibrate mortal vs. venial sins, such as buying papers online and submitting that as one's own [mortal sin!], copying others' work

---

[9] Rimer, Sara. "A campus fad that's being copied: Internet plagiarism." *The New York Times* (2003): B7.

without appropriate credit [mortal sin?], and merely neglecting to learn how to footnote properly [venial sin] (Jaschik, February 3, 2009).[10] We think the latter is a venial sin and Blum, correct about culture—Internet culture, that is, which believes that selecting, copying and pasting—and handing that in as a writing assignment (when little or no writing has been done)—is a root cause of educators' succumbing to online conventions rather than fighting those conventions. Neglecting to cite properly may be a venial, or easily forgiven sin; but the cumulative effect is more mortal than word theft because it undermines methodology, without which scholarship metamorphoses into newspaper copy: here one day, gone the next. Worse, easy arguments about online culture infected academe at a time when libraries were questioning what their role might be in a new media age. Many librarians saw their mission not as keepers of the literary keys but as "dissemination points" of data.

In the wake of such hoopla, several research teams came to notice that online citations were vanishing at increasing rates[11]. As the authors of this book work at an institution of science and technology, it was only natural that we observed that Internet footnotes "in cyberspace are like atoms in various states of decay"[12]. The phrase "half-life" was more than symbolic, however; it also described a type of radioactive de-

---

[10] Jaschik, Scott, "It's Culture, Not Morality." *Inside Higher Ed* http://www.insidehighered.com/news/2009/02/03/myword. 3 Feb 2009.

[11] Bugeja & Dimitrova, "The Half-life of Internet Footnotes Used in Communication Journals"; Dellavalle et al.; Taylor & Hudson; Tyler & McNeil.

[12] Carlson, Scott. "Here Today, Gone Tomorrow: Studying How Online Footnotes Vanish." *Chronicle of Higher Education* 30 Apr 2004: A33.

cay within a time period that could be measured as done with
isotopes in physics. Simply by measuring that decay in each
article published in each edition of a journal, we could estimate a decay rate to a specific publication and add to the body
of knowledge in our discipline yet another benchmark for citations apart from ones appearing in *Journal Citation Reports*.[13]

For us, this was a genuine moment of discovery that not
only applied to our disciplines, but to everyone else's, including the whole of the Internet. To be sure, we were not the
first to notice linkrot or even to measure vanishing footnotes;
moreover, a few prior studies even recommended solutions[14].
What distinguished our research was its implementation on a
cross-disciplinary scale in leading journals whose editors, by
and large, were not prepared for what would have to be done
to correct the phenomenon and preserve peer review and scientific method. One might have anticipated observations of
this sort to have emanated out of the sciences rather than social sciences. That is what we initially anticipated. However, as
we continued to publish studies on the phenomenon, we
came to see that our disciplines—journalism and communication—ultimately are responsible for upholding standards.

---

[13] Journal Citation Reports
(http://scientific.thomsonreuters.com/products/jcr/)
collects data on academic journal use and impact. Their measure
of cited half-life refers to the age of cited articles and their measure of citing half-life refers to the median age of articles cited in a
particular journal, both of which are very different from our half-
life estimation.

[14] Evans, Michael, and Steven Furnell. "The Resource Locator
Service: Fixing a flaw in the web." *Computer Networks* 37, no. 3-4
(2001): 307–330. See also Taylor, Mark, and Diane Hudson.
"'Linkrot' and the Usefulness of Web Site Bibliographies." *Reference and User Services Quarterly* 39.3 (2000): 273–277.

Across the disciplines, journal editors of every academic stripe work in our venue while preparing each year thousands of manuscripts for publication. Similarly, chairs of graduate programs across the disciplines do the same while reviewing dissertations for approval. These are editorial functions that track back to journalism and communication—which historically either reported scientific results so that they could be tested or disseminated those results through the various communication platforms.

There was another, more personal aspect as impetus to the focus of our research. Both authors of this book do research in new media and technology. As such, we cannot help but cite Internet-based sources—one of the reasons you will see digital citations in our footnotes here—because the foci of our scholarship are more often online than in articles and books. We typically encountered lapsed URLs, documents archived under different addresses, and some that simply disappeared never to surface again, even through searches in engines as expansive as those of Google or digital snapshots as detailed as those of the Wayback Machine. Simply by changing and renaming servers, computer technicians routinely destroy for citation purposes entire archives on a scale as disastrous as the legendary but mysterious fire at the ancient Library of Alexandria. "The loss of the ancient world's single greatest archive of knowledge, the Library of Alexandria, has been lamented for ages," writes historian and technology expert Preston Chesser. "But how and why it was lost is still a mystery. The mystery exists not for lack of suspects but from an excess of them"[15]. Chesser's statement is easily adapted to focus on what future generations of researchers may document:

> The loss of the modern world's single greatest archive of knowledge, the Internet, has been lamented for ages. But how and why it was lost is still a mystery. The mystery exists not for lack of suspects but from an excess of them.

We will unravel the mysteries of vanishing footnotes in upcoming chapters, reviewing the history of the effect and sharing our findings and recommendations.

---

[15] Chesser, Preston. "eHistory.com: The Burning of the Library of Alexandria." http://ehistory.osu.edu/world/articles/ArticleView.cfm?AID=9.   24 Oct 2009.

Chapter 3

A Brief History of Footnote Flight

The authors of this book have a few things in common in that we are prolific and write about new media and information technology. Michael Bugeja focuses on ethics across platforms and Daniela Dimitrova, the impact of new media on society. Bugeja's research is qualitative, Dimitrova's, quantitative, combining their talents and methodologies to publish a dozen individual or co-authored papers on how the footnote took wing on the Web and vanished from view. We are social scientists, not library ones, although we spent much of our graduate education in libraries and now visit real and virtual ones almost daily. So our view of the half-life of citation is that of the typical scholar in any discipline educated in the paper epoch: When we cite sources, we expect them to remain in the places we found them, whether that be a book or a blog. We do so out of transparent scholarship, ensuring current and future researchers that our literature reviews did not misrepresent a theory, that our methodologies took no shortcut, that our discussions advanced previous ones, and that our conclusions—based on all that came beforehand—might withstand the test of time. Time tests the footnote to determine the sturdiness of an argument, theory, or finding. That is why time is at the crux of our study documenting the half-life of Internet citations.

In assessing the significance of our research, we not only had to deal with the ephemeral nature of new media and the Internet; we had to understand the history of the footnote whose utility in the humanities, especially rhetoric[16], is to persuade and in the social and hard sciences, to prove[17]. We were not interested in the footnote as a vehicle of persuasion or authority because we were aware of how despots and demagogues used it in government dictums, religious tracks, royal mandates, and revolutionary manifestos throughout the ages. Buttressing an argument by citing a papal decree, for instance, might have held sway in 17th Century Italy (but perhaps not in 17th Century England, which broke with Rome). In sum, what persuades or empowers in one century (or even decade) may dissuade or disempower later or may vary according to culture and place. Rather, we were interested in the history of proof because evidence transcends argument from one century to the next and from one place to another.

Modern scholarship is steeped in proof, from literature review to future study. Moreover, that proof has rested for centuries on the modern footnote whose antecedents track to Erasmus' 1512 work, *On Copia*). Erasmus divided rhetoric into two categories, *expression of words* and *subject matter or ideas*[18]. Subject matter and ideas relied on experiment and analysis, giving rise to methods by Bacon (1561-1626) and later, Locke (1632-1704). Not lost on us upon revisiting the history of the footnote was the proliferation of the printing press during the lifetimes of those secular apostles of proof. Bacon and Locke depended on the firewall of the book to scrutinize the veracity of conventional thought in their search for verifiable truth.

---

[16] Burke, Kenneth. *A Grammar of Motives*. Berkeley, CA: Univ of California Press, 1969.

[17] Grafton, Anthony. *The Footnote: A Curious History*. Cambridge, MA: Harvard University Press, 1999.

[18] Bizzell, Patricia, and Bruce Herzberg. *The Rhetorical Tradition: Readings from Classical Times to the Present*. Boston: Bedford Books of St. Martin's Press, 1990. p. 504.

Bacon, in particular, helped reverse the pathway of truth from the deduction of Aristotle to the induction of observable method[19]. In this manner the factual footnote played a role in advancing science (and society) because it built a house of empirical truth, brick by brick. Those who doubted a theory, observation, or experiment could examine each brick as well as the method in which bricks were laid to verify assertions. Induction changed how humans perceived the world; it was a great leveler of authority, too, because truth knew no social class. As science advanced because of citation, deduction became as suspect and shaky as building the roof of a house before the floors, walls and foundation had been laid. Locke so distrusted the passionate, artful, persuasive, rhetorical methods of deduction that he dubbed them "perfect cheats"[20].

The transformation of method from deduction to induction set the stage for the next chapter of the modern footnote, which could not fully come into being without language being fixed through dictionaries. This occurred before the 18th century in France and Italy; and in the 18th century, in England and America. Each innovation—the printing press, which fixed text; the scientific method, which fixed fact; and the dictionary, which fixed language—was a stepping stone in our scholarly tradition, leading to citation method by Leopold von Ranke (1795-1886) who used footnotes to advance historical objectivity and scientific history. Over time, this defined scholarship as we know it today from primary source to peer review. In essence, the discipline of scientific history combined the exactitude of science with the sourcing of history, emphasizing the importance of primary sources[21]. By doing

---

[19] Ibid., p. 10.
[20] Ibid., p. 10.
[21] Grafton, p. 34.

so, von Ranke and others elevated the footnote as a required
component for replicability, which the erosion of Internet
footnotes undermines: It destabilizes fixed language, obfus-
cates the original source, and interrupts the inductive process.
In doing so, this effect not only reverses the focus on verifiable truths but indirectly empowers rhetorical expression and
even fake online information because links can be fabricated
as easily as they can vanish. The stability of citation is basic to
research, and if the Internet remains unstable, the implication
over time will mean that online scholarship will become a sec-
ond-class citizen in education and in the medical, social and
hard sciences. Our hope when we began our research in 2003
was to recommend ways to stabilize a fundamental component of research, so that future generations can investigate the
Web with the same reliability that previous generations en-
joyed in the book-laden library. Our initial study on this topic
examined papers of the Communication Technology division
of the Association for Education in Journalism and Mass
Communication (AEJMC), the flagship association for journalism educators.   We did this to see whether this problem
should be cause for concern in our discipline. The first study
used a convenience sample of papers from this academic division. We did it for good reason: No one had investigated the
phenomenon in our discipline as of that first study. Ordinar-
ily, a convenience sample is considered a preliminary way to
go about a scientific study; but that has more to do with the
long history of mass communication research since the invention of the telegraph. Research has been done online for a few
decades now, but during that time, few studies have analyzed
the nature of doing research online. Ours was among the first.
That is why we had to start from the beginning by asking a
seemingly pedestrian question: "Do footnotes vanish in papers by scholars of a technology-based discipline?" That ques-

tion in essence established the grounds for further in-depth study. As such, a convenience sample was appropriate because all a comprehensive study would have yielded is more of the same result, and the result was, that online citations were disappearing at an alarming rate. Some 40% of such citations had vanished within a year of the conference in which these papers were accepted. Next, we wanted to see whether the same was happening in the leading journals in our field. Before we embarked on the next phase of our research, it was important to review current research about the half-life phenomenon in other disciplines. Literature on online footnote decay is significant, but not focused on the big picture involving peer review and scientific method.

McMillan[22], for example, analyzed health sites on the Web from 1997 to 2000, finding that 27% of URLs disappeared after three years. She showed that sites created and maintained by private individuals tended to vanish at higher rates than those of government and education, which were more stable. Germain[23] analyzed 31 journal articles in the library sciences, finding about half of online citations were inaccessible after three years. During that same period she also discovered a trend indicating the number of articles with lapsed footnotes had increased from 38 percent to 68 percent. Casserly and Bird[24] studied the availability of Web-based footnotes in

---

[22] McMillan, Sally. "Survival of the Fittest Online: A Longitudinal Study of Health-Related Web Sites." *Journal of Computer-Mediated Communication* 6, no. 3 (2001): n. pag.

[23] Germain, Carol. "URLs: Uniform Resource Locators or Unreliable Resource Locators." *College & Research Libraries* 61, no. 4 (2000): 359-65.

[24] Casserly, Mary, and James Bird. "Web Citation Availability: Analysis and Implications for Scholarship." *College and Research Libraries* 64, no. 4 (2003): 300–317.

scholarly articles from 1999 to 2000, discovering that only 56% of those citations were still stable. Additionally, they learned that 81 percent of lapsed citations could be located after subsequent Web searches; 89 percent were available in the Internet Archive. Online citations in medical journals also were vanishing, as a recent study disclosed, analyzing references in three leading medical journals and finding that 13 percent of cited links were inactive after 27 months[25].

As more and more researchers from other disciplines discovered the same phenomenon that we did, few were able to forecast the implications for scholarship and research in the long term. That would become one of our tasks. The fact is, without reliable footnotes, scholarly journals—especially ones focused on new and electronic media—eventually may be discounted by researchers in years to come, no matter who was editor or how impressive the credentials of authors. Why should online research remain the understudy of paper-based research, we asked, especially since the Internet promised us a global village of erudition? Most scholars, even the most avid online ones, would rather publish their research in a paper journal rather than on a Web-only scholarly site. Why? What was it about paper that so mesmerized scholars? To illustrate that at the 2006 annual International Communication Association conference in Dresden, Germany, we brought a copy of one of the prestigious journals whose content is analyzed here. We showed the journal to the audience and then ripped out pages of an article, asking those in attendance how they felt in the pit of their stomachs. They ached for a simple reason: Ripping out articles from journals deprives other scholars of access to the material. That is why it is a crime to write on or cut and paste in journals in the library. The Internet enables

---

[25] Dellavalle et al.

copying, cutting, pasting and manipulating data. That remains the fundamental difference between exact copies of a printed journal or book, which we call the "ultimate fire-walled medium," and the Internet. Those who invented the latter for military purposes were not interested in maintaining the scientific method. Those who commercialized it were not interested in maintaining peer review. Thus, it is up to educators everywhere to repair a platform created to surveil and sell so that it can preserve and endure.

To do that, we have to assess the implications of our findings.

Chapter 4

The Half-Life of Online Footnotes

The more libraries invested in online databanks and digital journals, the more researchers were able to affirm findings of increasing use of online citations[26]. This was the first inkling that trouble loomed on the horizon for scientific method and peer review. Perhaps as much as medicine, law requires stable footnotes upon which to base new or amend existing litigation, especially with regard to appeals. A key component of the legal process concerns law reviews, where jurisprudence is explicated note by note to discern where the courts will be going next on an issue. Journals contain information that foretells the trajectories of future decisions. This is why editorships of such journals are considered coups d'etat. Rumsey in a random sample of law citation reviews found that online footnoting increased from 130 in 1995 to 5,462 in 2000, documenting how easy access can inflate citation with no promise of later retrieval.

Other disciplines have experienced the same phenomenon. Markwell and Brooks[27] documented disappearing footnotes in biochemistry. Kushkowski[28] noted that stability of online citations in print and electronic theses was poor apart from any

---

[26] Bugeja & Dimitrova, "Exploring the Half-life of Internet Footnotes"; Davis; Markwell & Brooks; Rumsey; Sellitto; Taylor & Hudson.

[27] Markwell & Brooks.

[28] Kushkowski, Jeffrey. "Web Citation by Graduate Students: A Comparison of Print and Electronic Theses." *Libraries and the Academy* 5, no. 2 (2005): 259–276.

academic field. Online citation practices by students were also disconcerting. Davis and Cohen[29] documented student use of such references rising from 9% to 21% from 1996 to 1999, respectively. Other researchers continued to chronicle the disappearance of online citations—in some cases, with more than half prone to failure. The researchers used different terms to describe the phenomenon—"link rot,"[30]; "persistency,"[31]; "persistence,"[32]; "availability of online sources"[33]; or half-life[34].

The authors of this book embraced the term "half-life" because it helped skeptics see how much can be lost in so little time. Our approach not only was to document that footnotes disappeared, but also to determine the factors that caused their disappearance. To do so we had to discern how frequently articles in our select journals used online citations. Then we looked at whether those footnotes emanated from top-level domains and how far down one had to click on a Web site to retrieve a text associated with a citation. We checked to see if the text that a footnote pointed to was accurate and whether the citation noted when the URL was retrieved. We also looked for the kind of error messages that

---

[29] Davis, Philip, and Suzanne Cohen. "The effect of the Web on Undergraduate Citation Behavior 1996-1999." *Journal of the American Society for Information Science and Technology* 52, no. 4 (2001): 309–314.

[30] Markwell & Brooks; Taylor & Hudson.

[31] Davis, Philip. "Effect of the Web on Undergraduate Citation Behavior: Guiding Student Scholarship in a Networked Age." *Libraries and the Academy* 3, no. 1 (2003): 41–51.

[32] Kushkowski; Rumsey.

[33] Casserly & Bird; Germain.

[34] Bugeja & Dimitrova, "Exploring the Half-life of Internet Footnotes"; Koehler; Tyler & McNeil.

non-working URLs displayed. We compared the content of journals dedicated to new media to that of traditional media journals. Finally, we tried to resurrect dead citations using Google and the Wayback Machine. This, we felt, not only would give us a snapshot of the half-life but also might indicate how scholars were using the Web for citation.

An increasing body of research documents how scholars use the Internet in their citations. The results are not pretty. For example, Harter and Kim[35] examined the availability of electronic resources among peer-reviewed electronic journals, finding that even in the same year, one-third of such citations were unavailable. Some studies reported a lower attrition rate, such as findings in the examination of Internet references in *New England Journal of Medicine, JAMA: The Journal of the American Medical Association* and *Science*, with only 13% inaccessible after two years[36]. Taylor and Hudson[37] studied the decay in Web site bibliographies and found that 30% of the links experienced "linkrot." Casserly and Bird[38] examined 500 Internet citations randomly chosen from scholarly articles published in library and information science journals, identifying that a mere 56.4% of those URLs were permanent, with the rest missing from the original Web address. Worse, as far as traditional academic standards are concerned, this study further noted that more than half of the online citations contained incomplete information; moreover, the majority

---

[35] Harter, Stephen, and Hak Kim. "Accessing Electronic Journals and Other E-publications: An Empirical Study." *College & Research Libraries* (1996): n. pag.

[36] Dellavalle et al.

[37] Taylor & Hudson.

[38] Casserly & Bird.

lacked reference to a retrieval date. Boynton and Imfeld[39] found decaying online references in popular public relations textbooks with an increasing number of inactive links -- from 17% in 2001 to 37% in 1998. Spinellis[40] examined the decay rates of online citations in two prominent computer science journals and found that 20% of them vanished within a year, with 10% more vanishing each year thereafter. Goh and Ng's[41] study reported that 31% of the URLs from three leading information science journals were inaccessible when tested. Sellitto[42] examined the permanence of Web citations in academic conference articles and found that 46% of the online sources could not be accessed. While some vanished citations could be retrieved via search engine or specialized archive, there was general agreement that complete restoration of vanished online links was not possible.[43]

[39] Boynton, Lois, and Cassandra Imfeld. "Virtual Issues in Traditional Texts: How Introductory Public Relations Textbooks Address Internet Technology Issues." *Journalism and Mass Communication Educator* 58, no. 4 (2004): 330–342.

[40] Spinellis, D. "The Decay and Failures of Web References." *Communications of the ACM* 46, no. 1 (2003): 71-77.

[41] Goh, Dion, and Peng Ng. "Link Decay in Leading Information Science Journals." *Journal of the American Society for Information Science and Technology* 58, no. 1 (2007): 15–24.

[42] Sellitto, Carmine. "The Impact of Impermanent Web-Located Citations: A Study of 123 Scholarly Conference Publications." *Journal of the American Society for Information Science* 56, no. 7 (2005): 695–703.

[43] Casserly and Bird; Harter, Stephen, and Charlotte Ford. "Web-based Analyses of E-journal Impact: Approaches, Problems, and Issues." *Journal of the American Society for Information Science* 51, no. 13 (2000): 1159–1176.

The analysis of online citation decay also gave scholars new concepts. In the first comprehensive study on the topic, in 1999, Wallace Koehler in the *Journal of American Society for Information Science* argued in "An analysis of Web age and Web site constancy and permanence" that Web pages in general exhibit two types of longevity behavior: constancy and permanence. Constancy refers to whether a Web page carries the same online content over time while permanence measures the probability of a Web page to carry the same URL over time[44]. However, Koehler's study focused on a random sample of generic URLs rather than a more focused analysis of the permanence of Web citations in academic journals, documenting the impact on methodology and replicability. Nonetheless, Koehler (1999) developed three categories for Web page permanence: always present Web documents, intermittent Web documents (which fail to respond but reappear over time), and "comatose" Web documents (those vanished from the URL). He documented a half-life of 1.6 years. In a later four-year longitudinal study, Koehler[45] found that the half-life of Web pages equaled two years. His studies concluded that Web page content becomes more stable over time and inferred that that the half-life of online resources differs across disciplines[46].

Online citation decay is defined as any digital footnote transitioning from being accessible to becoming inaccessible on

---

[44] Koehler, Wallace. "An Analysis of Web Page and Web Site Constancy and Permanence." *Journal of the American Society for Information Science* 50, no. 2 (1999): 162-180.

[45] Koehler, Wallace. "Web Page Change and Persistence: A Four-year Longitudinal Study." *Journal of the American Society for Information Science and Technology* 53, no. 2 (2002): 162-171.

[46] Koehler, Wallace. "Web Page Change and Persistence: A Four-year Longitudinal Study."

the Internet. Prior research has identified several areas of focus in online citation use and decay. The research areas include examining the characteristics of online citations, the frequency of use, and their decay rate. Matching content between online citation and references and the common error messages for non-working URLs have also been identified in prior research. Scholars have also looked at the possible predictors of online citation permanence, which include age of the online citation, presence of a retrieval date, top level domain, link hierarchy and academic focus of the journal[47]. Finally, some research has addressed the question of how to retrieve missing citations[48].

There is no doubt that online citations are becoming increasingly common in academic research. As the literature above showed, journal articles in a number of disciplines rely on Internet footnotes. A number of factors have been identified as predictors of online citation permanence. Predictors are defined as factors that significantly influence online citation permanence over time. We wanted to know just how they affected the vanishing act of digital citation, and we summarize those effects in the next chapter.

---

[47] Dimitrova, Daniela V., and Michael Bugeja. "Consider the Source: Predictors of Online Citation Permanence in Communication Journals." Dresden, Germany, 2006.
http://halfnotes.org/portals.pdf. 26 Aug 2009.
[48] Casserly & Bird.

Chapter 5

What, In Fact, Causes Footnotes to Vanish?

From our very first study of papers in our academic organization, we began to wonder why some footnotes survive while others don't. So we had to test which factors would emerge as significant predictors of online citation permanence. Other studies looking at the decay of online footnotes have consistently shown that older footnotes are more likely to become inaccessible when compared with newer ones. So many computer-based decisions can happen, from a new design of a Web site to a new server, or the migration of one database or publication from one institution to another. All the while, folks worried about making the transition and the new design, databank or publication accessible to the public. Because the people who make such decisions tend to specialize in computer science or programming, they just didn't give much heed to the importance of footnote stability. In any case we documented that there is a negative relationship between number of years since publication and citation accessibility. Others came to the same conclusion. Goh and Ng's[49] study documented that older Internet citations were less likely to be working than more recent citations. Tyler and McNeil[50] documented that the number of inaccessible citations increased over time. In 2006, in one of our dozen studies, the

---

[49] Goh and Ng.
[50] Tyler, David, and Beth McNeil. "Librarians and Link Rot." *Libraries and the Academy* 3 (2003): 615–632.

authors of this book did an empirical analysis of six journalism and communication journals, showing that the age of the citation was negatively related to online citation permanence. Studies in other disciplines continue to document a similar tendency. Therefore, we expect that older citations to be more likely than recent ones to become inaccessible.

Another predictor of online citation permanence identified in the literature concerns providing a retrieval date (i.e., when the online footnote was accessed on the Web). Note how we footnote online citations in this book. We include the date when we accessed the information. We had theorized that footnotes offering dates of retrieval are more likely to be stable than ones that don't. Research on this factor, however, was inconclusive, as we shall learn in later sections. Nevertheless, we generally recommend that article authors provide as much information about the citation as possible in order to find a missing citation in the future[51]. At the very least, the date may provide people using the Wayback Machine or other Internet snapshot applications a place to start, trying to retrieve a lost citation by checking what the Web looked like on the day an author reportedly accessed the URL.

Different online domains may be more stable than others. Previous research has shown that top level domain (TLD) is a significant predictor of online permanence. That term means the Internet page with the parent URL. For instance, check out our site dedicated to research on the half-life of Internet footnotes: http://www.halfnotes.org. The TLD in this case is ".org." If you access an article, or hotlink on our site, it will contain that root and add more words to the URL, as in http://www.halfnotes.org/our_history.html. Then there are the types of domains, including "com," which means "com-

---

[51] Rumsey.

mercial" and is the most common TLD. The extension, "org," represents "organization"; "net," also is for organizations; "edu," for educational institutions; "gov," for government entities. There are others, such as "biz" and "info," but ones listed earlier are the most common and extant for more than two decades.

Research similar to ours had been done before on TLDs. Tyler and McNeil[52], for instance, determined that *.gov* was the most stable top level domain. Koehler's study showed that both *.gov* and *.org* domains seemed to be more reliable than other domains[53]. Goh and Ng[54] (2007) also found *.org* URLs to be more stable when compared with other domains. This is consistent with our research, which found that *.org* and *.gov* were the most stable domains for online citations in journalism and communication. While there is some variation in previous findings[55], in general the studies tend to show that online footnotes in the *.gov* and *.org* domains are more stable than those in other top level domains. By the way, domains also have country designations, such as "fr" for "France;" but we did not test them specifically but included them and other extensions into a catchall category called "other."

Additionally, we and others found that the place of a Web page within the URL structure—in other words, URL *depth*, may affect online citation permanence. Spinellis[56], for instance, found a negative relationship between link hierarchy and link accessibility, with longer URLs being less accessible. In other words, increasing link depth was associated with

---

[52] Tyler & McNeil.

[53] Koehler.

[54] Goh & Ng.

[55] Koehler.

[56] Spinellis.

higher link failure. That's coincidental to computer science, we think. The higher the link in the hierarchy, the simpler the URL. So when links get too long, someone gets the idea to create a new folder and lump similar content there. The result? A failed footnote. Reasons aside, a similar finding was reported by Goh and Ng[57]. Tyler and McNeil[58] found that online footnotes that link to sub-files within a Web site performed worse than online footnotes that link to a home page, arguing that that long URL links to files deep into the server directory structure are less likely to remain accessible over time. Our study also showed that links to home pages were more likely to be stable. As a rule, homes should be stable, built on a firm foundation. The metaphor applies.

One of the specific measures of online citation decay is the half-life estimation. The half-life of online citations, as noted earlier, is defined as the time it takes for half of the online footnotes in any publication to become inaccessible.[59] By calculating the decay of articles in any one journal, the method also can estimate a decay rate for a specific publication. That data can be tracked annually by editors and organizations sponsoring publications.

---

[57] Goh & Ng.

[58] Tyler & McNeil.

[59] Some studies do not report the way in which they have reached a half-life estimation. We have reported the formula used for our half-life estimation in an earlier publication in *New Media & Society*, as follows:

$t_b = [t\ ln(0.5)]\ /\ [ln\ W(t) - ln\ W(0)]$ where t_b is the estimated number of years it takes for 50% of the published Internet citations to become inaccessible, $W(0)$ is the number of accessible online citations at the time of publication and $W(t)$ is the number of accessible online citations at a later time t.

Scholars from different disciplines have estimated the half-life of online sources in their areas, which range between 1.4 to 5 years. The lower the number, the more severe the decay rate. Goh and Ng, for example, found a relatively high half-life for online sources in information science journals: the estimated half-life was five years. In other words, it would take five years for half of the online citations in those journals to decay. The authors looked at articles published in the three leading information science journals over a seven-year period (1997-2003). Another study reporting a low half-life measure was conducted by Rumsey[60]. She examined the decay rate of references in law review articles and found their half-life to be 1.4 years (in other words, it would take 1.4 years for half of those online references to disappear). Harter and Kim[61] tracked only the first 20 references in 74 e-journals and found their half-life to be 1.5 years. Other scholars in other disciplines have shown perhaps more typical values of 2-3 years for the half-life of online sources.

With the technological revolution of the Internet, journals across academic disciplines have had to evolve and adapt. Most of the research on the evolution of journals and their adaptation to new technological platforms such as the Internet comes from the library and information sciences. Librarians, after all, have been responsible in the past not only for housing first and secondary sources in their archives, but for managing those archives and ensuring the retrieval of data within them. As such, veteran library scientists have been particularly interested in how traditional journals are adapting to the Web and whether any principles of scholarship would be

---

[60] Rumsey.

[61] Harter and Kim.

affected by online migration. Anderson[62] identified these five major adaptations or "mutations" for journals that transition to online platforms.

1. Shed volume, issue and page as document identifiers.

2. Abandon periodic publishing and publish as ready for immediate online dissemination.

3. Rethink sequence and primacy of the print era, especially in relationship to table of contents, lead articles and references to early online versions to the same publication. In other words, when we eliminate periodic publishing, suddenly the format of a table of contents changes, along with information noting where and when an article has been published, and whether it is showcased as a major piece. This will entail more checking by viewers to make sure that they have accessed the most current version of a piece. In sum, the trend is to allow the platform to determine how data is sequenced and accessed.

4. Mutate the archive, and participate in this mutation, worrying less about the constancy and permanence of data stored there and more about upgrading, correcting or otherwise revising what is stored there.

5. Evolve to your readers' expectations about networked journals, allowing the audience rather than the editor to dictate standards.

Among the multiple challenges that the Internet brings to academic publishing is the use of online footnotes in research

---

[62] Anderson, Kent. "The Mutant Journal: How Adaptations to Online Forces Are Forcing STM Journals to Mutate." *Learned Publishing* 14, no. 1 (2001): p. 22.

publications. One of the goals of this book was to investigate how journal editors of top mass communication journals have adapted to Internet-based footnotes. It is important to report how journal editors themselves perceive and deal with the practice of using online sources in the publishing of academic research since they play an important role in the adoption of any new editorial policies.

We examine all this plus report findings in upcoming chapters.

Chapter 6

Opinions Versus Reality: Journal Editors and Vanishing Footnotes

The goal of this book was to extend our previous research and document not only the half-life phenomenon comprehensively, but also discern what can be done to lessen the impact of the deterioration of online footnotes. We focused on the top journals in journalism and communication in order to (1) evaluate the characteristics of the online footnotes used, (2) estimate their decay rate, (3) measure the influence of multiple predictor variables, (4) provide editorial insights into the phenomenon, and (5) present general recommendations for journal authors and editors facing the half-life issue. The journals were *American Journalism, Human Communication, Internet Research, Journal of Broadcasting and Electronic Media, Journal of Communication, Journal of Computer-Mediated Communication, Journalism & Mass Communication Quarterly, Journalism History,* and *New Media & Society.*

In earlier chapters we identified several characteristics of online footnotes that are important to examine and a number of factors that affect citation longevity. Based on those concepts, our work attempts to answer the following questions:

Question 1 and Related Issues

- What is the general profile of online citations used in journalism and communication articles?

- What is the frequency of use of Internet citations in refereed research articles in journalism and communication journals?
- What are the most common domains in the online citations?
- Are the online citation sources hyperlinked correctly?
- Do the online citations provide retrieval dates?

Question 2 and Related Issues

- How many online citations remain accessible over time?
  - What is the half-life of online citations in articles in journalism and communication journals?
  - What is the expected decay rate?

Question 3

- What is the relationship between journal focus and online citation permanence?

Question 4 and Related Issues

- What are the views of journal editors about the half-life phenomenon?
  - Do the journal editors believe that the decay of online citations is a serious issue and, if so, what are their views regarding the use of online citations in academic research articles?
  - What kinds of policies, if any, exist to guide the use of online citations in each journal?

o   *Is there any association between type of journal and level of concern/awareness about this phenomenon?*
o   *What is the role of journal prestige and journal longevity in editorial opinions?*

A total of 2,305 online footnotes were analyzed. The URLs were accessed in late 2006 to check if they were still accessible. The data show a steady increase in the use of online footnotes over time: 419 (18.2%) of the online references were published in 2000 articles, 462 (20%) in 2001 articles, 680 (29.5%) in 2002 articles, and 744 (32.3%) in 2003 articles. The frequency of use of Internet citations across journals varied over the four-year period, with the *Journal of Computer-Mediated Communication* having the highest number of online citations (653) and *Journalism History* the lowest (22). The distribution of online references per journal is shown in Table 1 in Appendix D. Not surprisingly, history journals rarely made use of online sources. The journal with the highest percentage of working citations -- 60.3% -- was, again, the *Journal of Computer-Mediated Communication* while the journal with the lowest percentage was, again, *Journalism History* with only 36.6% working citations.

Question 1 also asked about the most common domains in the online citations used in the nine journals. The results show that the generic .*com* domain had most citations (739, or 32.1%), followed by .*org* with 559 (24.3%), .*edu* with 396 (17.2), and .gov with 179 (7.8%). The category "*other*" contained 432 (18.7%) of the citations. Based on the coded data, it is not possible to distinguish what kind of organizations were referenced in the .*com* citations.

Also related to Question 1, we checked what percentage of the online citation sources were hyperlinked correctly, i.e. contained no errors in the URL address. The data show that the vast majority of URLs were correct; only 10% of the 2,305 were not hyperlinked correctly. In terms of retrieval dates, also related to Question 1, only 1,071 (46.5%) of the online citations provided a retrieval or access date. It should be noted, however, that not all citation guides require the authors to do so.

Question 2 asked how many online citations remained accessible over time. Our results indicate that only 1083 (47%) of the 2,305 citations worked when checked in late 2006. The majority of the online citations (53%), however, were inaccessible. The next step in the data analysis was to conduct a half-life estimation of the decay rate. Again, half-life was defined as the time (in years) it takes for half of the online citations in a journal to become inaccessible.

As shown in Appendix D, the average half-life of online citations in journalism and communication journals was estimated at 3.95; in other words, it would take roughly four years for half of the online citations used in the nine journals to disappear from the Web. The data show that the half-life was highest for online references in the *Journal of Computer-Mediated Communication*, which was established at 5.97, followed by *American Journalism* with a half-life rate of 5.59. The lowest half-life was estimated for the online references in *Journalism History* (half-life value of 2.67), followed by *New Media & Society* (half-life value of 2.94). Thus, the expected decay rate varies by journal. A higher percentage of accessible online sources corresponds to a higher half-life, which leads us to conclude that JCMC's performance was superior.

To examine the differences between different types of journals, the nine journals were divided into two groups: new media and traditional journals. The new media journals included the *Journal of Computer-Mediated Communication*, *Internet Research*, and *New Media & Society*; the rest were coded as "traditional" journals. The type of journal was included as a dummy variable in the logistic regression analysis reported below but was not significant. To answer Question 3, there was no statistically significant difference in online citation permanence between traditional and new media journals.

One factor that affected online citation permanence was year of publication. The accessibility of online citation decreases gradually from 2003 to 2000. Our calculations also indicate that compared with publication year 2003, the probability of online citations from year 2002 to remain accessible decreases by 24%. In other words, citation decay increases over time.

Providing a retrieval date for the citation was expected to be positively related to online citation permanence. This expectation was not supported by statistical analysis, indicating that online references become inaccessible regardless of whether or not authors provide access dates. Indirectly, this finding suggests that the volatility of online information cannot be avoided even when special care is taken to provide exact retrieval dates.

Our methodology also revealed that, when compared with the category "other," *.edu* and *.gov* are more likely to contain working citation than the other domains. This finding suggests that the significance of TLDs may be dependent on the field of examination (e.g., journalism versus aerospace engineering).

Lastly, we expected that online citation permanence would be negatively related to the URL level of the citation. We found that citation links to level 1 URLs (i.e., home pages) remain most stable relative to the other URL levels.

What did the journal editors think about all this? Our last research question asked about editorial views on the half-life phenomenon and inquired if the journal editors believed that

the decay of online citations constitutes a serious issue for
journals to address. Despite the number of cross-disciplinary
studies documenting the half-life problem, including studies in
our field, their views reveal that many do not acknowledge the
seriousness of the issue.

*New Media & Society, Journalism & Mass Communication Quarterly, Journal of Communication, American Journalism, Journalism
History*, and *Journal of Internet Research*, all reported that they
have not experienced this problem. However, both *New Media
& Society* and *Journal of Internet Research* check online citations
for link decay before printing an article. It is interesting to
note that *New Media & Society* and *Journalism & Mass Communication Quarterly* do not think there is a need for a special policy,
or that this is a particular problem facing journals. *JMCQ*, in
particular, is noted as one of the top journals in mass communication primarily because of its reliability and prominence in
areas of research. It would seem decay of online citations
would be a high rather than a passing priority. Conversely,
*Journal of Communication, Journal of Internet Research, Journal of
Broadcasting and Electronic Media*, and *Journal of Computer-Mediated
Communication* all agree that online citation permanence is a
problem, and some sort of policy should be established. In
short, about half of the journals had experienced the problem,
and most of the editors interviewed thought that something
needed to be done about it.

We also asked about the editorial views regarding the use of
online citations specifically in research articles. Regarding academic research, most of the editors agreed that using the Internet for academic research was fine, as long as the sources
were reputable. Most agreed that personal homepages and
sites such as Wikipedia were not to be considered reputable,
accurate sources of information. *Journal of Communication* and
Journalism & Mass Communication Quarterly specifically men-

tioned personal home pages as unacceptable. *American Journalism* mentioned blogs and Wikipedia as unacceptable, and *Journalism History* mentioned Wikipedia as unacceptable.

Question 4 also asked a related issue concerning editorial policies established to guide the use of online citations in each journal. Of all the journals in our sample, only one reported to have a special policy: the *Journal of Internet Research*. (However, the journal does not expound on what that particular policy is. An examination of the website, as recommended by the journal, produced only information about how to format online references. No formal or informal policy on using online citations was readily available on the journal's Web site). Another interesting case is the *Journal of Computer-Mediated Communication*, which is an online-only journal. It encourages people to use online references and also links for graphics and multimedia elements in their articles. That journal also provides some tips for finding more "long-lasting" links. Interestingly, JCMC was also the journal with the best citation "half-life." The rest of the journals examined here -- *Journalism History, American Journalism, Journal of Communication, New Media & Society, Journal of Broadcasting and Electronic Media* and *Journalism & Mass Communication Quarterly* did not have any formal policies or informal recommendations about using online references at the time our studies were concluded. That said, *Journalism History* notes that it will reject any papers that have "too many" online citations.

We also asked the editors whether there is any association between type of journal and level of concern/awareness about online citation decay. Three of the four "technology focused" journals--*Journal of Computer-Mediated Communication, Journal of Broadcasting and Electronic Media,* and *Journal of Internet Research*— seemed to be aware of and concerned about the half-life problem. *New Media & Society* was the exception. All, again excluding that journal, included checking online citations specifically to make sure they are accessible at the time of publishing. All, excluding *New Media & Society*, believe that the half-life issue is a real problem, and that something should be done about it.

In contrast, the other journals barely seem aware of the problem. None have any specific rule to check online citations, other than making sure the format of the citation is correct according to whatever style guide they use. The *Journal of Communication* is the most concerned, and believes that there should be some sort of policy as they have already experienced the problem of vanishing online citations. *Journalism & Mass Communication Quarterly, American Journalism,* and *Journalism History* have never experienced this problem, and do not seem very concerned about it happening. Indeed, *Journalism & Mass Communication Quarterly* asserts that online citations are generally inconsequential to the manuscripts. JMCQ's editor does not perceive any real difference between online citations and citations to regular print materials. *Journalism History* and *American Journalism* both said that they receive very few articles with any online citations in them anyway. This confirms some of our previous assumptions and analyses that history-oriented research relies more on primary sources and rarely on online ones, at least for the time being.

Finally, we inquired whether journal prestige and journal longevity play a role in editorial opinions and attitudes toward online footnotes. The findings here do not show any clear distinctions between more and less established journals as well as newer and older journals.

In terms of journal prestige, the *Journal of Communication* and *Journalism & Mass Communication Quarterly* are ostensibly the two most "prestigious" journals in the field. However, they have fairly different views regarding the half-life phenomenon. *Journal of Communication* is fairly progressive, believes this is a serious problem, and thinks that something should be done to fix the problem, such as introducing a special policy. *Journalism & Mass Communication Quarterly,* on the other hand, does not think this is a real problem, and does not think anything really needs to be done. Surprisingly, the editor says that he has never encountered this problem and has never heard of it before.

In terms of journal longevity, the nine journals rank as follows, from oldest to newest: *Journalism & Mass Communication Quarterly* (1924), *Journal of Communication* (1951), *Journal of Broadcasting and Electronic Media* (1956), *Journalism History* (1974), *Human Communication Research* (1974), *Journal of Internet Research* (1991), *American Journalism* (1991), *Journal of Computer-Mediated Communication* (1995), and *New Media & Society* (1999). It becomes hard to make any particular assertions about journal longevity. For example, *Journal of Communication* is much older than *New Media & Society,* yet the views of the editor at *JoC* seemed more progressive toward the half-life phenomenon than *NMS,* who did not believe this was a real problem that required a special policy. Also, the *Journal of Broadcasting and Electronic Media* thought that this problem required a policy as well, and this is one of the older journals, compared to *Journalism History* or *American Journalism,* both of whom have never faced this problem, and do not think that online citations are growing. In general, journal longevity does not seem to drastically affect editorial opinions.

When it comes to the question about whose responsibility is it to ensure the preservation of online reference material that may eventually vanish from the World Wide Web, there is no consensus. *New Media & Society* and *American Journalism* would like to see a not-for-profit or maybe a governmental group to emerge that attempts to keep track of material that may vanish or has already vanished. *Journal of Internet Research*

thinks it is the responsibility of the Wayback Machine to preserve online content. The rest of the editors do not have specific suggestions in this regard. When asked what authors, editors, and publishers should do concerning disappearing online
citations, most of the journal editors responded, "I don't
know." The *Journal of Computer-Mediated Communication, Journal
of Internet Research,* and *New Media & Society* said they should try
to preserve as best they can. *Journal of Internet Research* gave
specific advice—detail citations with date viewed and keep
copies of cited material. While there was very little agreement
among the editors about who is responsible for mitigating the
phenomenon, the only commonality was that nobody thought
it was the editor's job to solve the half-life phenomenon.
That attitude alone is reason enough for readers of this
book to follow our rationale and recommendations in the
final chapter.

Chapter 7

An Online World as Thin As It Is Wide

Our studies have been able over time to identify key factors that affect the stability of online footnotes in journals in our disciplines. Our findings in the last chapter showed that three factors are significant in predicting online citation permanence: year of publication, URL hierarchy and top level domain. Specifically, older online references were less likely to be available; home page links were more likely than longer links to be accessible; and *.edu* and *.gov* links were more stable than other domains. Our findings are consistent with research in other areas[63]. The results indicate that these three characteristics of online citations should be considered when authors and editors evaluate the integrity of sources for their articles and published works.

The stability of online footnotes has always wavered the longer data remained online, as our findings document again. This effect continues to worsen as online citations have been used now for several years, undermining fact checks and statistical comparisons or follow-ups of earlier watershed studies in our most prestigious journals. Again, this is why we are concerned about peer review and the health of scientific method, especially now, as traditional media platforms such as print are being used less and the Internet more.

The more the Internet is used, the more computer scientists and programmers pay homage to the deity of the server and

---

[63] Casserly & Bird; Goh & Ng; Markwell & Brooks; Sellitto; Spinellis.

the angelic order of the file folder system. They need a re-
minder about the sanctity of an archive that remains in one
place, in real life or in cyberspace. Archives are as precious
now as they were in the time of ancient Alexandria, perhaps
even more so, because we are inventing on borrowed time in
the name of innovation. Without archives, we reinvent the
wheel. This notion is lost (along with archives) whenever media outlets and publishing companies decide to incorporate a
new design on the Internet. That this could happen in 2009 at
The Chronicle of Higher Education, cited in this book and thousands of journal articles and Web sites, is a case in point.
When notified that former URLs of its archive had been lost
with its design upgrade, the company realized its error and
redirected as many links as possible to previous content. But
as more and more writers, including a co-author of this book,
incorporated URLs in content published in *The Chronicle*, those
links went dead, too, and were never restored. As such, linkrot
in the digital age is apt to happen in a new digital hierarchy
beyond the scope of this book but related to one of our findings concerning top-level domains. Lost URLs of articles may
be restored or redirected to reassemble an archive, but if the
content of those articles contained embedded links—as is cus-
tomary in the digital age—chances are those links also will
vanish. In sum, a Web redesign as happened at *The Chronicle*
can kill hundreds of links embedded in content, including
perhaps the most important section of any article: footnotes.

The loss of archives, URLs and embedded new media have
consequences for all journals, even media history ones. It
comes as no surprise to us that findings show increasing use
of online footnotes over time in all our selected publications,
with 419 of the online references in 2000 articles increasing to
744 in 2003 articles. Also as anticipated, the frequency of use
of Internet citations across journals varied, but ranged pre-

dictably with the *Journal of Computer-Mediated Communication* having the highest number of online citations (653) and *Journalism History* the lowest (22). Studies of computer mediated communication by nature would have to focus on the Internet and, in turn, cite online sources many of which, over time, vanish. A media history journal would tend not to focus on the Internet but the print and still photography sources of the past—a fact that will change in time when future historians will want to research new media and online innovations. Media history, of all genres of mass communication research, may be affected most by the half-life phenomenon because its methodology rests upon primary and secondary sources. Now it must consider a new specter in its primary methodologies: ephemeral sources that are here one day, gone the next. Also, as anticipated, those doing research about the Internet would tend to know the most reliable online data and domains. This, too, was borne out with *Journal of Computer-Mediated Communication* boasting the highest percentage of working citations, 60.3%. Interestingly, the journal with little need to use the Internet also had the lowest percentage of working citations, 36.6% as found in *Journalism History*.

However, when the most common domains were considered collectively, it disappointed us that the most common domain in the online citations used in the nine journals was the generic *.com*. If anything, this finding convinced us that editors of journals in our disciplines need to heed basic research about online footnotes and scrutinize authors who use a top-level domain meant for commerce. That commerce in media typically also means that a newspaper or broadcast outlet with archive news available via subscription, again killing the original online citation and replacing it with a 404 error or advertisement to subscribe before one can download the original document. The more stable *.org*, *.edu* , and *.gov* followed in that order, with the catch-all "*other*" category containing 432 (18.7%) of the citations.

The data did allow us to estimate a collective half-life rate of 3.95 years, as only 1,083 (47%) of the 2,305 citations worked when checked in late 2006. The majority of the online citations (53%) had vanished. We would like to have thought that journals whose authors seemed to recognize online stability were ones publishing in a discipline requiring Internet content; but that was both proved and disproved by the journals with the longest and shortest half-life rates in the book. The *Journal of Computer-Mediated Communication* had the highest rate but was followed by *American Journalism*. The lowest half-life rate was associated with *Journalism History*, followed by *New Media & Society*. We cannot make any broad-ranging claims about why this is so; but it does prompt the question of whether editorial guidelines concerning online citations would be useful in every journal.

Our research looked in depth into how the type of journal impacted its half-life. To examine that effect, we separated journals into two groups, or new media and traditional journals. The former was represented by *Journal of Computer-Mediated Communication, Internet Research*, and *New Media & Society*; the rest were classified as "traditional" journals. However, there was no statistically significant difference in online citation permanence between traditional and new media journals. This may suggest that different editors add their personal influence with a host of external reviewers who may or may not pay heed to the half-life effect.

One of the surprising findings concerned the inclusion of "retrieval dates," which had no bearing on the likelihood of a citation lapsing into the digital void. We are aware that not all footnote reference guides recommend retrieval dates, and their inclusion from a technical perspective would have little bearing on whether a digital citation lapsed or remained stable. But we recommend the retrieval date from an editorial perspective in that it can aid in the hunt for vanished source material through use of the Wayback Machine and/or other archives or methods. Even in the fact-checking of URLs in this book, we encountered an essential one that had vanished from the Georgia Institute of Technology, which reformatted part of the URL named after its "Graphics, Visualization - Usability Center" (abbreviated "gvu") to the more recent "College of Computing" (abbreviated "cc" in the URL), essentially undermining links to some of its early computer surveys that constitute an important early digital archive and requiring a few days of detective work on our part to ascertain not only where the link had gone but also what "gvu" and "cc" meant. More important, the retrieval date on the lapsed URL played a key role in identifying the original source document.

As the above anecdote shows, our results beg the question whether technology is a self-determining organism ("an end in itself") transforming anything it touches "while being scarcely modified in its own features," as Ellul[64] has observed. This could be inferred from the last hypothesis that predicted online citation permanence would be negatively related to the URL level of the citation. The data indicated that the lower in the URL tree directory, the more apt a citation was to lapse, with the odds of a level 1 (home page) citation working increasing by 182% over a level 7. From a technological perspective, this simply suggests that lower Web site levels are affected by changes in folder system or file designation in levels above it, with the greater number of levels above it pos-

---

[64] Ellul, J. "The 'Autonomy' of the Technological Phenomenon." *Philosophy of Technology: The Technological Condition.* Ed. Robert Scharff. Malden, MA: Blackwell Publishers, 2003.

sessing increasing odds of file or format changes. Again, what happened at *The Chronicle of Higher Education* in its 2009 redesign, is a practical example of that effect.

Editorial perspectives provided some additional insights to our book. However, we found some viewpoints remarkable given the fact that almost everyone using the Internet experiences missing URLs and the leap to that effect on footnoting, peer review and scientific method is not a great one. As reported, *New Media & Society, Journalism & Mass Communication Quarterly, Journal of Communication, American Journalism, Journalism History,* and *Journal of Internet Research,* all stated that their publications had not experienced the half-life phenomenon to be problematic. The fact that *New Media & Society* and *Journal of Internet Research* do check online citations for linkrot suggests that content alone (in contrast to media history journals) had compelled them to undertake this practice. Again, we found it curious that *New Media & Society* and *Journalism & Mass Communication Quarterly* do not believe there is a need for a special policy or that vanishing online citations is a problem. Editors provided no empirical evidence to the contrary, and it would be inappropriate for us to speculate as to why they felt this way. *JMCQ,* in particular, is noted as one of the top journals in mass communication in large part because of its reliability and research prominence. In as much as its online submission guidelines go into detail on footnoting, with 13 examples of first and second reference use (para. 7, "Basic End Note Style," n.d.), one would postulate that decay of online citations would be of high enough importance to merit a mention there rather than passing priority. Finally, we inquired whether journal prestige and journal longevity play a role in editorial opinions and attitudes toward online footnotes. The findings here do not show any clear distinctions between more and less established journals as well as newer and older journals.

Moreover, as the case with *JMCQ* illustrates, journal prestige in the end essentially had little to do with views concerning the half-life phenomenon. Happily, *Journal of Communication* acknowledges the impact on scholarship and believes a special policy should be created to address the half-life effect. Finally, we were gladdened to learn that *Journal of Communication, Journal of Internet Research, Journal of Broadcasting and Electronic Media,* and *Journal of Computer-Mediated Communication* agreed that permanence of online citations was an issue that required some sort of policy.

We also believe that collectively, editors of these publications will be forced to deal via policy or guidelines with the half-life effect. While most editors said use of online citations was acceptable, as long as the source was reputable, a few singled out blogs, personal home pages, and Wikipedia as unacceptable. Reputable or not, the fact is that these categories of sources all share a common trait: content often disappears or changes over time, especially in Wikipedia, whose content in some entries changes hourly. While the Wikipedia listing may be stable, as well as the URL, depending on the entry, the content can vary substantially with assertions non-verified remaining and morphing into variants that sully peer review and scientific method. That presents some citation challenges.

Finally, we were somewhat disheartened to learn that there was no consensus on whose responsibility it might be to ensure preservation of and access to online references in danger of vanishing from the Web. That lack of consensus led us to publish this book because authors will be held responsible when footnotes in their articles no longer can be located, a situation that can generate anything from a negative review to allegations about invention.

What can be done? We only have partial solutions. Previous studies on online citation decay have tried to identify recommendations for scholars to reduce the severity of the half-life phenomenon. Goh and Ng[65], for example, offered the following recommendations for extending this: Avoid long URLs; cite documents found in digital collections on the Web rather than Web sites in general; attempt to repair broken links manually; and use "friendly" URLs (i.e., easily remembered and understandable). None of these recommendations, however, addresses the underlying problem of vanishing online sources.

Some new services that attempt to aid in link preservation also exist. Hitchcock and others[66] discuss *The Open Journal Project* link service, which calls for authors contributing to online journal publications to verify links before adding them to the document. As we write there are new media companies that promise to archive content upon which links are based. Also, organizations have also attempted to create solutions to the half-life problem. Some archive only academic research, others archive different types of online content, and others allow authors to create back-up copies of digital documents themselves. However, none of the current systems seems to be doing the job of preserving digital content in a comprehensive manner. Neither do these services have control over vanishing online links in general. Our goal was to restore the firewall of the journal and book to the Internet so as to trust the foundation of online research.

One potential solution—basing use of online citations not on HTTP protocols but on a Digital Object Identifier system

---

[65] Goh and Ng, p. 23.
[66] Hitchcock, Steve et al. "Citation Linking: Improving Access to Online Journals." *Proceedings of the second ACM international conference on Digital libraries.* 1997. 115–122.

(a digital barcode whose permanence would also authenticate content)—has gained some but not enough currency since our studies began tracking the problem in 2004. As we have noted in previous studies, the challenge here is essentially market-based rather than scholarly. This is in keeping with the history of technology such as occurred with the 1980s competition between Sony's Betamax recording system and JVC's Vertical Helical Scan (or VHS) recording system. (Beta tapes were smaller and preferred from a technical standpoint, but JVC's marketing push won out.) As their Web site states, the DOI system offers "framework for persistent identification" of digital content and is managed by the International DOI Foundation, which has both "commercial and non-commercial partners." To learn more about Digital Object Identifiers, see http://www.doi.org.

We end this book with recommendations that may help in the short term until the collective of scholars and researchers realize the impact on scientific method and make serious attempts to establish permanent digital archives in the public interest. As we have in previous studies, we continue to advise using print sources whenever possible or pdfs of articles as long as they remain in library databanks. A printed article in journal or chapter in a book remains the ultimate "firewalled" medium. A pdf is a photograph of that paper article or chapter. Although it can be reformatted as an altered pdf, we doubt that will occur in a library databank. That said, we remain skeptical that pdfs will continue to be offered to libraries by such vendors as ProQuest precisely because the format is not easily altered and students and scholars prefer text or html so that they can select, copy, paste and reformat at will. Of course, once a pdf is reformatted, even if content is not altered, the dimensions of page setup or the choice of a new font effectively ruins the accuracy of the citation, as pages are

renumbered or graphs and statistics located in different rows
or columns of tables. In 2005, during a half-life experiment,
we found that ProQuest's delivery of html-formatted documents adds a space when the URL runs from the left to the
right side of the page, killing the URL. We encourage readers
of this book to urge scholarly organizations and librarians to
retain pdf format. As discussed earlier, researchers should
note the retrieval date (no matter what style) as one additional
piece of information to help track vanished URLs.

Colleagues who serve as graduate school directors, journal
editors and peer reviewers need to be made aware of the half-
life effect so that students and contributors understand the
ramifications of vanished footnotes. They also can be enlisted
to help find solutions to mitigate the effect. Colleagues, editors, students and reviewers also need to appreciate why con-
certed effort has to be made to lengthen the stability of online
footnotes. A good starting point would be to know terms
such as constancy, permanence and half-life as well as the
most and least reliable domains used in online citation.

Ultimately, we feel, the best single technology available today remains DOIs -- digital object identifiers -- but previously
discussed shortcomings will continue to plague that option or
any other viable alternative until scholars put a higher pre-
mium on footnote stability. This is why we are noting the
larger ramifications of peer review and scientific method. The
only other viable recommendation we can make after years of
analyzing the effect in scholarly journals is to assemble a task
force from members of leading academic organizations such
as the Association for Education in Journalism and Education, the International Communication Association, the National Communication Association, the American Media Historians Association and other interested organizations to join
ranks in advocating for a DOI or other universal system and,

in the meantime, to require their publications to formulate policies acknowledging the half-life of Internet footnotes and informing contributors and reviewers about factors that exacerbate or mitigate the effect.

Our feeling is that DOIs have the potential to alleviate the management of information in a digital environment, but organizations and publications will tend not to use them universally. True, there are open-source libraries and archival Web sites, several of which allow programmers to add code with the potential to impact the stability of footnotes. But these are fleeting attempts to address a phenomenon that affects the whole of scholarship on the World Wide Web at a time when society faces global dilemmas that only threaten to worsen over time, including issues of food, fuel, water, disease and climate. Without the scientific method in place to address them, scholars will experience setbacks that could have been avoided if only more attention were paid to the sanctity of footnotes in preserving archival knowledge. At a time when most online scholars in the academe advocate for sustainability, we find it curious that they overlook the sustainability of citation and the ramifications for an online world without them.

Works Cited

Anderson, Kent. "The Mutant Journal: How Adaptations to Online Forces are Forcing STM Journals to Mutate." *Learned Publishing* 14, no. 1 (2001): 15–22.

Bizzell, Patricia, and Bruce Herzberg. *The Rhetorical Tradition: Readings from Classical Times to the Present.* Boston: Bedford Books of St. Martin's Press, 1990.

Boynton, Lois, and Cassandra Imfeld. "Virtual Issues in Traditional Texts: How Introductory Public Relations Textbooks Address Internet Technology Issues." *Journalism and Mass Communication Educator* 58, no. 4, (2004): 330–342.

Bugeja, Michael, and Daniela V. Dimitrova. "Exploring the Half-life of Internet Footnotes." *Iowa Journal of Communication* 37, no. 1 (2005): 77-86.

---. "Implications of Vanishing Online Citations." *Journalism and Mass Communication Educator* 62, no. 2 (2007): 212-218.

---. "The Half-life Phenomenon: Eroding Citations in Journals." *The Serials Librarian* 49, no. 3 (2006): 115-123.

Bugeja, Michael, Daniela Dimitrova, and Hyehyun Hong. Online Citations in History Journals: Current Practice and Views from Journal Editors. *American Journalism* 25, no. 4 (2008): 83-100.

Burke, Kenneth. *A Grammar of Motives*. Berkeley, CA: Univ of
     California Press, 1969.

Carlson, Scott. "Here Today, Gone Tomorrow: Studying
     How Online Footnotes Vanish." *Chronicle of Higher
     Education* 30 Apr 2004: A33.

---. "Scholars Note 'Decay' of Citations to Online Refer-
     ences." *Chronicle of Higher Education* 18 Mar 2005: A30.

Casserly, Mary, and James Bird. "Web Citation Availability:
     Analysis and Implications for Scholarship." *College
     and Research Libraries* 64, no. 4 (2003): 300–317.

Chesser, Preston. "eHistory.com: The Burning of the Library
     of   Alexandria."   http://ehistory.osu.edu/world/
     articles/ArticleView.cfm?AID=9. 24 Oct 2009.

Davis, Philip. "Effect of the Web on Undergraduate Citation
     Behavior: Guiding Student Scholarship in a Net-
     worked Age." *Libraries and the Academy* 3, no. 1
     (2003): 41–51.

Davis, Philip, and Suzanne Cohen. "The Effect of the Web
     on Undergraduate Citation Behavior 1996-1999."
     *Journal of the American Society for Information Science and
     Technology* 52, no. 4 (2001): 309–314.

Dellavalle, Robert et al. "Going, Going, Gone: Lost Internet
     References." *Science* 302, no. 5646 (2003): 787-788.

Dimitrova, Daniela V., and Michael Bugeja. "Consider the
     Source: Predictors of Online Citation Permanence in

Communication Journals." Dresden, Germany, 2006.
http://halfnotes.org/portals.pdf. 26 Aug 2009.

---. "Exploring the Use of Online Citations in an Online-only
Journal: A Case Study of the Journal of Computer-
Mediated Communication." San Francisco, CA, 2007.
http://www.allacademic.com/meta/p_mla_apa_rese
arch_citation/1/6/9/4/3/p169430_index.html.

---. "Raising the dead: Recovery of Decayed Online Citations." *American Communication Journal* 9, no. 1
(2007): n. pag. http://acjournal.org/holdings/
vol9/summer/articles/citations.html. 26 Aug
2009.

---. "The Half-life of Internet References Cited in Communication Journals." *New Media & Society* 9, no. 5
(2007): 811-826. Sage Journals Online.
http://nms.sagepub.com/cgi/content/abstract/9/
5/811. 26 Aug 2009.

---. "Vanishing Act: The Continued Erosion of Online Footnotes in Communication Journals." Montreal, Canada,   2008.   http://www.allacademic.com/meta/
p_mla_apa_research_citation/2/3/0/9/8/p230985_i
ndex.html. 10 Sep 2009.

Ellul, Jaques. "The 'Autonomy' of the Technological Phe-
nomenon." *Philosophy of Technology: The Technological
Condition.* Ed. Robert Scharff. Malden, MA: Blackwell
Publishers, 2003.

Evans, Michael, and Steven Furnell. "The Resource Locator
    Service: Fixing a Flaw in the Web." *Computer Networks*
    37, no. 3-4 (2001): 307–330.

Germain, Carol. "URLs: Uniform Resource Locators or Un-
    reliable Resource Locators." *College & Research Librar-
    ies* 61, no. 4 (2000): 359-365.

Goh, Dion, and Peng Ng. "Link Decay in Leading Informa-
    tion Science Journals." *Journal of the American Society for
    Information Science and Technology* 58, no. 1 (2007): 15–
    24.

Grafton, Anthony. *The Footnote: A Curious History.* Cambridge,
    MA: Harvard University Press, 1999.

"GVU's Eighth WWW User Purvey: Problems Using the
    Web   Graphs." http://www.cc.gatech.edu/gvu/
    user_surveys/survey-1997-10/graphs/use/Problems
    _Using_the_Web.html. 24 Oct 2009.

Harter, Stephen, and Charlotte Ford. "Web-based Analyses of
    E-journal Impact: Approaches, Problems, and Is-
    sues." *Journal of the American Society for Information Sci-
    ence* 51, no. 13 (2000): 1159–1176.

Harter, Stephen, and Hak Kim. "Accessing Electronic Jour-
    nals and Other E-publications: An Empirical Study."
    College & Research Libraries 57 (1996): 440-456.

Hitchcock, Steve et al. "Citation Linking: Improving Access
    to Online Journals." *Proceedings of the Second ACM In-
    ternational Conference on Digital Libraries.* 1997. 115–122.

Jaschik, Scott, "It's Culture, Not Morality." *Inside Higher Ed*
    http://www.insidehighered.com/news/2009/02/03/
    myword. 3 Feb 2009.

Kaufman, Paula. "Scholarly Communication: Library Leaders
    Press Colleges to Archive Online Journals to Avoid
    Loss   of   Data   Archives."   24   Feb   2006.
    http://www.library.illinois.edu/blog/scholcomm/arc
    hives/2006/02/library_leaders.html. 19 Jan 2010.

Koehler, Wallace. "A Longitudinal Study of Web Pages Con-
    tinued: A Consideration of Document Persistence."
    Information Research 9, no. 2 (2004): n. pag.
    http://informationr.net/ir/9-2/paper174.html. 26
    Oct 2009.

---. "An Analysis of Web Page and Web Site Constancy and
    Permanence." *Journal of the American Society for Informa-
    tion Science* 50, no. 2 (1999): 162-180.

---. "Web Page Change and Persistence: A Four-year Longi-
    tudinal Study." *Journal of the American Society for Infor-
    mation Science and Technology* 53, no. 2 (2002): 162-171.

Kushkowski, Jeffrey. "Web Citation by Graduate Students: A
    Comparison of Print and Electronic Theses." *Librar-
    ies and the Academy* 5, no. 2 (2005): 259–276.

"Library." *The New Encylopaedia Britannica.* 15th ed. Chicago:
    Encyclopaedia Britannica.

Markwell, John, and David Brooks. "Broken Links: The
    Ephemeral   Nature   of   Educational   WWW

Hyperlinks." *Journal of Science Education and Technology* 11, no. 2 (2002): 105–108.

McMillan, Sally. "Survival of the Fittest Online: a Longitudinal Study of Health-related Web Sites." *Journal of Computer-Mediated Communication* 6, no. 3 (2001): n. pag.

Nardini, Bob. "Invisible Links." *Academia: An Online Magazine and Resource for Academic Librarians* (2005). http://www.ybp.com/acad/features/0705_bugeja.html. 26 Aug 2009.

Rimer, Sara. "A Campus Fad That's Being Copied: Internet plagiarism." *The New York Times* (2003): B7.

Rumsey, Mary. "Runaway Train: Problems of Permanence, Accessibility, and Stability in the Use of Web Sources in Law Review Citations." *Law Library Journal* 94, no. 1 (2002): 27–39.

Rychkov, Cheryl. "Medieval Manuscript Production." 2003. http://library.rmwc.edu/hours/production.html. 10 Mar 2006.

Sellitto, Carmine. "The Impact of Impermanent Web-Located Citations: A Study of 123 Scholarly Conference Publications." *Journal of the American Society for Information Science* 56, no. 7 (2005): 695–703.

Spinellis, Diomidis. "The Decay and Failures of Web References." *Communications of the ACM* 46, no. 1 (2003): 71-77.

Taylor, Mark, and Diane Hudson. ""Linkrot" and the Useful-
     ness of Web Site Bibliographies." *Reference and User
     Services Quarterly* 39, no. 3 (2000): 273–277.

Tyler, David, and Beth McNeil. "Librarians and Link Rot."
     Libraries and the Academy 3, no. 4 (2003): 615–632.

Appendix A. Methodology

This book uses qualitative interviews and quantitative content analysis methodology. This is the culmination of our research and presents data collected since 2004, some of which have been reported previously in various venues. In this manuscript, we have added an online-only journal and two history journals to increase the representation of different sub-areas. Now we have a comprehensive dataset of nine journals that range from print to online journals and from historical to new media focus.

It should be noted that this book is based on data from a four-year period: 2000-2003. All articles published between 2000 and 2003 in the leading journalism and communication journals were retrieved using different online databases. The full-text articles from the following journals were saved and analyzed for online footnotes: (1) *American Journalism*, (2) *Human Communication Research*, (3) *Internet Research*, (4) *Journal of Broadcasting & Electronic Media (JOBEM)*, (5) *Journal of Communication (JoC)*, (6) *Journal of Computer-Mediated Communication (JCMC)*, (7) *Journalism History*, (8) *Journalism & Mass Communication Quarterly (JMCQ)*, and (9) *New Media & Society (NMS)*. These journals were selected because they are considered to be the most prestigious peer-reviewed journals in the field. They publish research from multiple sub-areas, including journalism, history, human communication research and electronic and new media. Several of these journals also are affiliated with leading associations such as the International Communication Association (ICA), the Association for Education in Journalism and Mass Communication (AEJMC), and the Broadcast Education Association (BEA). Another criterion used in the selection of the journals was their ISI impact factor from Journal Citation Reports (JCR).

The four-year period of publication years was chosen for analysis for several reasons. The first reason is the tangible increase in the number of online citations used in academic journals since 2000. Second, selecting a four-year time frame allowed us to track down and compare the use and decay of online citations use over time. The item in each study was the online footnote—i.e., each cited URL in the selected journal articles.

The population of all journal articles was downloaded starting in June 2004 and continuing until November 2006 when the history journal articles were added. Trained graduate student coders accessed all articles and recorded the exact URL address for each Internet source. Online citations that were repeated in the same article or appeared as ibid were excluded. Only research articles were selected for analysis. All other types of publications such as editorial notes or book reviews were excluded. Occasional URLs that were provided in the body of the article and not in the bibliography/ reference section were excluded since they serve a different purpose.

The coding instrument included several categories of interest. The two main variables were online citation *constancy* and online citation *permanence*. Permanence refers to the question whether the URL is accessible or not while constancy refers the question whether the content of the URL is the same as the content cited in the original online reference. Both of these variables were coded as nominal yes/no variables. The main dependent variable analyzed in this book was permanence (i.e., accessibility of the online citation), which was tested in 2006. The other categories included in the content analysis were year of publication of the article (2000, 2001, 2002, or 2003); retrieval date provided for the online citation

(0/1), if provided the exact retrieval date were also recorded; top-level domain (TLD) (.com, .edu, .gov, .org, and other domain, which included country domains); URL level (level 1 -- i.e., home page, level 2, level 3, etc. as illustrated in *http://level1/level2/level3/level4/leveln*; links to level 7 and higher were collapsed into one category); whether the URL was hyperlinked correctly (0/1); and presence of a '%' sign in the URL (0/1). Coders also recorded the exact error message for broken links and then classified it according to type of error: 400 (bad request), 401 (unauthorized access), 403 (forbidden or connection refused by host), 404 (page not found or file not found), 502 (service temporarily overloaded), 503 (service unavailable), or other. Level of agreement averaged .94 for all variables based on Holsti's intercoder agreement formula. The agreement ratings were considered acceptable.

Additionally, we conducted interviews with the journal editors of the selected journals between spring and fall 2007. The semi-structured interviews included a list of 14 questions aimed to capture the editorial views on use of sources in general and online citations in particular. The questions also asked about current journal policies regarding online citations and prior experience with decaying citations as well as responsibility for online content, which allowed us to answer the last research question. The interview was designed to allow flexibility for the editors who could participate either by phone or by email. An open-ended question at the end of the interview asked for any additional comments or feedback. The interview protocol is provided in Appendix B.

Appendix B. Interview Protocol for Journal Editors

1. If your responsibilities as a journal editor include examining the reference list of your accepted articles, do you pay special attention to online citations? Why? Why not?

2. In your journal, have you experienced the problem of using online citations that disappear at a later time? If yes, what did you do in this case (remove citation, introduce new policy, try to locate original via Google, some other action?). If not, why?

3. What is your perception about the frequency of use of Internet references in your journal articles? How about the use of online reference in scholarly work in general?

4. To what extent do you think the use of online references is acceptable in academic research?

5. Do you think online references are acceptable in order to get (or inspire) a research idea?

6. To achieve empirical (or practical) data to support the arguments?

7. Does your journal have any criteria for recognizing more stable URLs for citations? For example, do you have any preference in using online references in particular TLD such as .gov/ websites? What about personal homepages versus peer-reviewed research published online?

8.   What do you think is the difference between history-oriented journal and the other scholarly journals in communication in terms of online reference use?

9.   Why do you think the online citation is relatively rare in history-oriented journals compared with other areas in communication?

10. Does your journal have a particular formal policy or informal recommendations about using online references?

11. Whose responsibility should it be to ensure the preservation of online reference material that may eventually vanish from the World Wide Web?

12. Do you think it would be necessary to establish a special policy regarding the use of online reference? Or, do you think it is not necessary to worry about the phenomenon of disappearing online citations?

13. What should authors, editors, publishers do concerning disappearing online citations?

14. In closing, who do you think is responsible for solving the half-life phenomenon?

     Any additional comments you'd like to make?

Appendix C. Summary of Half-life Estimates in Previous Research

Study	Discipline	Sample/ Focus	Number of URLs Studied	Estimated Half-Life (in years)
Dimitrova & Bugeja (2007)	Journalism and Communication	Five leading journals, four-year period (2000-2003)	1,126	3.17
Goh & Ng (2007)	Information Science	Three leading journals, seven year period (1997-2003)	2,516	5
Harter & Kim (1996)	Peer reviewed e-journals from Sciences, Social Sciences, Humanities, and Professional areas.	74 e-journals from 2005, looked at the first 20 references in each e-journal article	83	1.5
Markwell & Brooks (2002)	Biochemistry and Molecular Biology	Three biochemistry class Web sites linking to scientific information sites, 13-month period (Nov. 2000-Dec. 2001)	515	4.6
Rumsey (2002)	Law	Law review articles, 100 per-year, 4-year period (1997-2001)	5,057	1.4
Sellitto (2004)	Education & Research Training	Conference proceedings, nine-year period (1995-2003)	1,068	4.8
Spinellis (2003)	Computer Science	Two journals, five-year period (1995-1999)	4,224	4.0

Appendix D. Online Citations per Journal with Half-life Estimation

Journal	Accessible Online Citations	Inaccessible Online Citations	Total	Half-Life
American Journalism	16 (53.3%)	14 (46.7%)	30	5.59
Human Communication	20 (40%)	30 (60%)	50	3.91
Internet Research	197 (41.6%)	277 (58.4%)	474	3.47
JOBEM	114 (41%)	164 (59%)	278	3.04
Journal of Communication	50 (49%)	52 (51%)	102	4.53
JCMC	394 (60.3%)	259 (39.7%)	653	5.97
J&MC Quarterly	120 (45.5%)	144 (54.5%)	264	3.45
Journalism History	8 (36.6%)	14 (63.6%)	22	2.67
New Media & Society	164 (38%)	268 (62%)	432	2.94
Total	1083 (47%)	1222 (53%)	2,305	*Average*=**3.95**

[a] The half-life estimation is based on 2006 data for citation accessibility.
[b]Half-life is defined as the time (in years) it takes for half of the online citations in a journal to decay.

Index

About the Authors

Michael Bugeja is a professor and the director of the Greenlee School of Journalism and Communication at Iowa State University of Science and Technology. He is the author of 21 books, including *Living Ethics across Media Platforms* (2008) and *Interpersonal Divide: the Search for Community in a Technological Age* (2005), both published by Oxford University Press and both of which won the Clifford G. Christians Award for Research in Media Ethics. *Interpersonal Divide* analyzes what happens to interpersonal skills on residential campuses and communities when we spend too much time consuming media and using technology. *Living Ethics* calls for a moral convergence to accompany the technological one.

Dr. Bugeja's commentaries on media ethics and technology have been cited internationally in such outlets as *Newsweek*, *The New Yorker*, *The New York Times*, *The Washington Post*, *The Christian Science Monitor*, *USA Today*, *The Guardian* (UK), *Toronto Globe & Mail* (Canada), *Die Welt* (Germany), *China Daily*, *The International Herald Tribune* (France), *The Ecologist* (UK), *The Futurist* and the Associated Press as well as online news editions of CBS, NBC, ABC, CNN, MSNBC and Fox News. He also writes regularly for *The Chronicle of Higher Education*. His scholarship has appeared in such academic journals as *Journalism Quarterly*, *Journalism Educator*, *Journalism and Mass Communication Educator*, *Journal of Mass Media Ethics*, *New Media & Society*, and other peer-reviewed publications in journalism and library science. In addition, he is a creative writer and winner of a National Endowment for the Arts fellowship with publications in *Harper's*, *Poetry*, *Georgia Review*, *Kenyon Review*, and *Sewanee Review*, among others.

Daniela V. Dimitrova is an Associate Professor in the Greenlee School of Journalism and Communication at Iowa State University. She received a Ph.D. in Mass Communication from the University of Florida in 2003. Dimitrova teaches classes in *International Communication*, *Political Communication*, *Multimedia Production*, and *Communication Technology and Social Change*. Her research interests focus on the impact of new media technologies, comparative journalism studies and the news framing of political events. Dimitrova's scholarly record includes more than 30 peer-reviewed publications. Her articles have appeared in the following journals: *The Harvard International Journal of Press/ Politics*, *International Communication Gazette*, *Journalism Studies*, *New Media & Society*, *Journal of Computer-Mediated Communication*, *Social Science Computer Review* and *American Behavioral Scientist*. She is a member of AEJMC, the largest U.S. organization for journalism educators, and most recently served as Head of its Communication Technology division.

Breinigsville, PA USA
19 October 2010
247564BV00002B/2/P